boy maybe

boy maybe

poems

W. J. LOFTON

BEACON PRESS, BOSTON

BEACON PRESS
Boston, Massachusetts
www.beacon.org

Beacon Press books
are published under the auspices of
the Unitarian Universalist Association of Congregations.

28 27 26 25   8 7 6 5 4 3 2 1

This book is printed on acid-free paper that meets the uncoated paper
ANSI/NISO specifications for permanence as revised in 1992.

Text design and composition by Kim Arney

Library of Congress Cataloging-in-Publication Data

Names: Lofton, W. J., author.
Title: boy maybe : poems / W. J. Lofton.
Identifiers: LCCN 2024040071 (print) I LCCN 2024040072 (ebook) I
ISBN 9780807017821 (paperback) I ISBN 9780807017814 (ebook)
Subjects: LCGFT: Poetry.
Classification: LCC PS3622.O386 B69 2025 (print) I
LCC PS3622.O386 (ebook) I DDC 811/.6—dc23/eng/20240911
LC record available at https://lccn.loc.gov/2024040071
LC ebook record available at https://lccn.loc.gov/2024040072

In Loving Memory of
Willie, Katheryn, and Lanita

For My Brother Willie,
I Know You're Out There Somewhere.

Contents

Preface

boy maybe: a queer artifact/anti-colonial weapon/survival psalm that signals my location in thought/soul/body. *boy maybe:* a hymn for hands who have known the pleasures and pains of touch and its absence, particularly for those who know themselves as queer/ Black/*other* while enduring unfreedom in its many modes: state violence/labor exploitation/racial terror and the ever-daunting task of confronting one's own self/imagings/limitations. Love/ through the dense sea of my own grief/was the lifeboat that rescued me/a boy drowning under the weight of phantom parents/anti-Blackness/and a secret large enough that legislation had to be drafted then *passed* to make one of the ways I love *legal. boy maybe*: evidence that I did not die when I thought I would or wanted to. At this moment in time I remain steadfast in denying the lies this country and its imperial cruelties have attempted to seduce me with, the age-old tales that I am alone/ unwanted/powerless. Reader, these words have found you, as the words of Jericho Brown, Danez Smith, Audre Lorde, and countless others found me.

boy maybe: a claim against the colonial binaries, patriarchal visions, and technologies of senseless yet intentional violence. In earlier drafts of this collection the cynosure was the over-whelming absence of lovingness. Desire appeared as a panting dog would, begging for water from anybody willing to pass it a bowl with a molecule of moisture at its bottom. I was subdued by the idea that grief without any hope of recovery was at minimum marketable material. I know now, although honest attempts, those poems were thin, one-dimensional, and self-deprecating. The poems *in* the following pages wanted more from me. *Demanded more than I could ever have imagined.*

Touch is used as a vehicle of radicalization. As the through line throughout this collection it is a utility for questioning and directing. *Is it here that aches?* Feel for it until you feel it, until you've dug to the root. I didn't want to be what people used to call me before I could name myself: fag, sissy—soft. One is not born into wanting anything but to live. *boy maybe* is my attempt at understanding who I am beyond the hatred I was taught to feel about myself. As James Baldwin put it, I had to vomit up all the filth.

I still am.

here today, gone today

the ditch
               spits
back the body.

the body
               decides
trying is prayer.

here today.

                              gone in a fl—

once-wack jokester

               wakes
into whirlwind.

shakes glass from skin.

tires burst.

shakes men

from skin.

driver's side
               dented.

       rain.

dresses   sharp,

post-crash

knife-like,

fashion butcher.

boy may be boy

survives everything

announced as final.

decides dying

is prayer

                    headed

toward rest.

and away from

his favorite lover

playing catch no longer

here today

                            gone in a

after each death

I watch rain
pluck cobwebs spiderless
watch what makes drowning possible
an opened throat
panic then more panic
I wait,
     I am always waiting
the names never illuminate the dark.
Mommy is dead. Daddy is dead.
           no.
    just taking their time to make up for old times.
    just stopping by the store for buttermilk to soak the chicken.
no.
    there's traffic. google-gossip: slowdown on I-90
no.
Love, fell on top of them.
                    after each death I think
           I'll attend my highschool prom again
and this time the polaroid snaps my hand around a boy's waist.
          around a boy's waist I've thrown my arms
              and prayed, "Don't leave."
       I'll beg for better things.
I'll beg for time back.
I'll beg for breakfast if that's what it takes.
I promise I won't get mad if the bacon burns.
I promise I'll let you watch me fall
       in love
and bring you another son.
I promise this rain is not impossible.
I promise I won't panic.

dreamhouse

me? an ocean of arteries. blood vessels. wind wrapped in wool.
cartoons watch me. a boy? maybe. borrowed Barbies in my
blooming. Buffy aficionado. broke boundaries with t-shirt
wig. beyond heaven's imagination. dreamhouse. dog walker.
dying to touch my mother's cheek; promise to remember this
go-round. she was? wooden box holding water. unquenchable.
loyal needle wielder in the 80s. weigher of 8 children. all: too
heavy. one given by her father. burden on top of bruise. black
like me. I am? sore. spoonful of funeral song. grief gong loud.
can't remember what they sang. just my father's face. eternally
painted still. I look just like my daddy. otherworldly. dressed
in my best going-out clothes. heel clicker. concert-goer. comet
gazer. cremains of my mother a meteor around my siblings'
necks. I am? ready now. teeth brushed. showered. hair
ponytailed. dog walked. dying. dreamhouse. driving to a new
city where my blood ain't used for diary ink, dirge, curbside
dinner for police——disinfectant for another man's living.
me. from the beginning? ocean. blood. wind. boy maybe.

gravity reports:

Mama is fighting gravity & bacon greases Sister's lips.
down the hall, Big Mama's knees Sunday-sag. says she prayin for
some relief & winning the lottery. mustard-seed faith she calls
it—asks us how we beg Jesus. asks us are our knees involved?

we report:

we'd make the dirt move. thunder telephones lightning & buys
us a minute with God. prayer feels like rain at first. feels like
an ocean being planted & unplanted. drowning & undrowning.
memories meticulous as ants in a meadow. Mama is fighting
gravity.

Mama reports:

the latch is maggot-covered then lifts the lid. everyone is
offered laughter in this poem: the hands reaching for bacon,
brother-sister, saint & sinner & scratcher of the ticket. Mama's
wizened mandible wiggles words: *I love you.*

> she falls down. she returns to God like
> Big Mama, to her knees.

to know touch better

still we were faggots before & after they killed us
we could have punctured the frog's curse sooner
my nigga's lush lips could have drawn neck-near
unknotting my durag with his row of neat white teeth

we could have punctured the frog's curse sooner
essex, jimmy, langston—sit knee-near, listen children, let me
    tell you bout these niggas
unknotting my durag with their rows of neat white teeth
niggas fade napes to know touch better

essex, jimmy, langston — i have nothing to give but my body
does this darkness remind you of anything?
niggas fade napes to know touch better
we were still in love after the church called us abominable

does his darkness remind you of anything?
Richard Pryor pressing *pleas* into his partner's ear
he was still in love after the church mothers called them
    abominations
the pastor begs for the faggots' dollars and shakes the glitter
    off: acting a fool for no reason

Richard Pryor pressing pleas into his partner's ear
his breath a blade of begging
the pastor begs for the faggots' dollars and shakes the glitter
    off: acting a fool for no reason
still we were faggots before & after they killed us

many things

there was a rock in his stiletto,
      small as a tear across the heart,
the night we wrinkled

sheets & offered walls gossip.

front porches leaned
      in our direction. the neighbors would later say,

drums, there must have been drums.

we have done many things; split, spread,
      been made over, been face down
& ass up. been fucked up & fucked over.

been tired.

been hungry. been nights without sleep.
      riding through Mississippi we fogged his car
on the side of a gas station.

we tasted waistlines.

we wanted to live.
we had reasons to be alive.

nipples lifted inside
      hoodies, slick
nickels.

property

gold
feathers
gold
hoop earrings minus
one
gold
not there
around the collar
of the bull's bully
bought by boys bending in bed
bamboo style
or less sturdy
like belts smacking
fresh out-the-shower asses
the buckle silver & walmart-bought
begs for blood in the language
of bayonets
around the collar
a circle of silver
a bone hanging
a name meaning scar in Swahili
a name meaning good boy
good riddance
don't you dare leave
to the one who gives it
& to the four legs that answer

the world is a world
of calls & commands
sit
lay down
turn over
come here
stay there
good boy
darling bitch your coat shines
brighter than scars
on a slave's body
on a woman's body
on a body not called to gender
reader which of us
has seen a body freed
gold dimmed
to yellow gold
gold given
between gentlemen
instead
of flowers

for Cadarius, Keith & Miles

45° stiff
armed anxious to make death grunt—an AR stiff
at our sides. strapped over our chests.

fatigue fell on us years later. under God

we crawled
through   our mothers and our mothers' fears
crawled   through cherry-stained mud,
crawled   through money too slim to pour milk, a means
            to an end.
crawled   knees past skin limits.

stripped me down.
    stripped you down.

made me pledge
   made you pledge   an allegiance to deathmaking.
                       an allegiance to tank-riding and
                       nation-tilting.

how'd we survive the smoke?
how'd we escape the factory?
                       I made a home in you where
                       bullets can't reach.
                       you made a home in me where
                       our enemies can't see.

Brother, I know what they did to you.
I wore the flag blowing backwards in the wind too.

I promise we never have to mention
_____ again.

or the times we laced our boots and marched in the opposite
direction of our families. I promise never to mention
_____ again.

pinky   swear. there are other wars to talk about.

to keep the flies away

pennies float in bags of water, count by twos
keep flies from touching what belongs to God

a mother cries over what belongs to God
and what her body knows belonged to her

anchor the night, no sun belongs to her
anchor her child in red clay and brown dirt

boys in heaven kick up red clay and brown dirt
what is the definition for hell, they ask

men will kiss in high water, for hell they ask
death reminds love of all her questions

death reminds us of all our questions
now sing, my lord knows my name

the lord Jesus knows my name
our names are called; He counts by twos

for Tae

Jesus is.   break—eat.
pour—drink.   more than
a suggestion.   aproned He strolls through
the kitchen   stirring soup
softer than   bird bones.
domestic savior.   stigmata can't grip
steam   but held death tight
close as new lovers   dancing.
He whispers   I love you.
every childhood shank turns over
like an engine.   i want to be responsible.
i want to rescue the boy   in the lake swallowing
mouthfuls of Alabama   catfish. his mother's boyfriend
pushed him in   rumors repeated.
he was plump   full of water   graying without age.
Jesus! Jesus! Jesus!   his grandmother moaned.
where'd the time go?
why *her* boy touched wet by some man?

using

hibisci   dye
shirts sweat soaked   antique pink   generous

citizens   en garde

give way to touch
flesh-theft   using   trumpets
held by us
boys close to Black   out drunk   stumble through doors
home to each other

bugles bounce against walls

against walls shirts wilt with moisture   peals pipers pick

petals from each   other's throats.

```
dominium
```

under

God's
chapped lips sighing

under

      sky
      opening into more sky

under

        horses
        afire

under

       a church
       darkened by dead light

under

                                    alabama's lazy
                                    eye

under

                              powerlines
                              producing no power
                              touch strikes

under

a shared blanket
between cousins

under

his breath
he does not have to whisper
what is known

under

his mother's roof
his hands are allowed
to be anything toward
me:
steel
hooks
bullets—whistling
toward game

under

the hill
heat borrows
flesh &
replaces it
with a scar.

pig

ask me, was the yolk broken at breakfast? ask me

what was the cost of filling the tank? which nation was the oil
siphoned from, then numbered in barrels?

how can bodies lie like logs for hours, beheaded across oceans,
without the beheading being made punishable?

why did the road to the diner provide ditch after ditch after ditch?
who did I not imagine ~~myself hating~~ upon my arrival there?

the woman across the table with my next month's mortgage in
her purse. the woman shares

that her father was a sheriff and the type of sheriff who didn't kill
people. people were the reason he took pride in his job. people

like you. people like me. he was a modest man appointed with
an alcoholic father. a father cursed with seeing beauty

only in architecture. apple blossoms were absent around the
house although they lived in a small town in Michigan.

I share that I was born in Chicago. the winters were brutal. she
shares more of her frostbitten childhood too.

who knew we both were too busy surviving? who knew, even then,
the ground beneath us shook with the brutality of mad butchers?

what did I do next? I ate bacon. I couldn't touch the toast. when
did I lose my mind?

petting the dog

abandonment is a practice. he pets the dog but not you. go practice. across town a man pleases himself. small possibilities cover his chest. make his hair sticky as licorice. your face is not in his fantasy, but unknowingly, he has passed your scent sitting on various department store counters. at this hour where do you imagine love to be? under the shower's head bathing. perhaps near one of Death's beds holding a hand curved with cancer. would you consider wilding yourself with wonder or unbraiding Fear's rope to reach out and find the center inside of you?

when your touch went
missing i remembered

holding myself for an eternity
formless
prior to flesh crawling over bone
spilled galaxies
cried out my own name and caught it with what was not yet a hand
sweet mercy how'd we forget
the questions we answered with our own touch.

first time we met

it was a double date
you with him
me with him
a table too small to catch your jokes
from spilling on everything
felt a secret growing
in us
in us
felt a secret growing
fear sunk the bones in his face
I know that now
I still see
the chandeliers swinging
in your eyes when I returned
from the bathroom announcing
I'd walked into the glass
and everyone laughed
some silently
imagining the pain
because they could imagine it
I'd been dazed
And crashed into the mirror
I had to pinch myself
I had to look you in the eye
and tell the truth
I'd run into my reflection

sweet

Today the police do not murder the boys.
They are already slipping out of their clothes.
When no one is looking,
They dance to Afro-Caribbean music
And pretend they are anywhere
ripe with mangos.

They lead a revolution,
Loosening buttons.
A whimper. A moan
Sounds haunt their bodies.
Pleasure is a sweet ghost.

It makes soldiers weep.
It makes men brave
To touch in public.
To be certain as the scent of blood.
The boys do not want the empire.

They see
What it is doing to their friends.
They hear
What is not being said. There are sirens blaring
On the other side of town.

right hooks

dare we discover everything while slow dancing
hips keep us from falling in halves but not apart
two angels wrestle & God names it dancing
two shadows stand feet apart
one whispers
we gon be alright
puts a hook in jaw
shadow on wall whines
shadow on floor
has no gag reflex
next comes nectar
over fences blocks away bees burp honeysuckle
men sit three words apart
in an abandoned parking lot
in an abandoned neighborhood
in a country abandoning its children
the car's speakers falsetto
I could hate you now, it's quite alright
tigermoths jig on car's hood
wings wide as radio frequencies
I've been dreamin', dreamin'
& again dancing in the holy
dark

language

we language. we sex numb. bodies shimmer wet prayers.
we unwrap legs and the sky shares its face with a corner
    of the ceiling.

fan spins in the same direction after you leave—after everyone
    leaves,
clockwise and lonely. our mouths wander roads upward, wet.

tongues knife blades of spit—a moist scar.
dry riots are forbidden. deemed not a language. we language.

we break bruises into white noise. take, eat. this is my body,
    which is broken
for you. it becomes too much not to touch a boy that leaks.

we leak a storm alive. we touch and wake up in the mouth of
    a dream.
we dream inside the other's mouth and slip into a song:
    you're gorgeous but you can't fly.

we dance. a fire races us home.
bodies shimmer after silence replaces everything.

our legs unwrap and the sky becomes a lid across the eye.
stars float above our vision.

below we took teeth from the mouth of our zippers
and inserted language.

we are a language that dances when everyone is asleep.
god always sees us. falling in love, over and over again.

half brutal

reaching begins in the heart—raising past tank tops &
plaid shirts. paddles through sunlight & chilly mornings.
in a parking lot full of humvees, lovers say see ya later when
goodbye feels too solid of a reality. oceans are crossed.

      breath goes in. breath comes out.

futures are being told. God traces meaning down backs & over
each head draws a star. spills sunshine over the enslaveds' kin.
ties thighs across fresh timber. Texas is where it happened:

      miracles riding the wind. love recognizing itself

& ordering one margarita with two straws. understanding
crawls into chests: life must only be half brutal. over the boys
roses grow. thorns sprout later.

      they scent drunk. they hips dip. they feel good. they hurt
      bad. they ask God what joke He is making out of them.

boxes are packed. tape tears in rain-colored slices. a new
apartment asks to be named home. a new boy burrows under
the sheets. a birthmark is shared.

      there is laughter archived in memories. laughter sails
      whistle-quick & stumbles through their shoulders.
      earths quake. homes tumble.

counting

my mother grips her dress
a man holds her hips
my life depends on their touching
it is 1992 on chicago's south side
they sit on December's edge
counting kisses
four on the shoulder
three on its blade
two for the body not yet a body
she turns him inside out
plants her feet in his lap
like sand pressing around
a laughing child's neck

dark

home is dark, in its dark, I place mine:
poked-at, played-with, I retrace lines.

       safety having been signed for, I trace lines.
       it hurts knowing where hurting hides,

under my dark, against the dark, hurt hides.
I shake off someone's touch.

       pretend it's the opposite of someone's touch.
       mother, big brother did terrible things.

brother, our mother hid terrible things.
she left, without us, one Sunday night.

       a boy left, without me, on Sunday night.
       in a white car not ready for long distance.

each boy I love, readies for distance.
home is dark, in its dark, I place mine.

polka dots

that's not his heart
it's the Honda's
muffler missing
situated passenger side
the pillow's
polka dots
design distance
between you and
winter sleep
chill kisses everything
the black spade
tucked deep
backseat somewhere
inside December
ghosts in every
shade stare
at us
driving nowhere
in circles
polka dots
pressed against
time's face

fire eats

God's   sobbing|laughter|mercy

settles in us

the way   reflections|tossed coins|pilots   hover

above water

in a blur bridges abandon standing

cheeks swell   with what ifs|sunflower seeds|lies white &
                      little lips protrude

eyes widen at   children split by adoption |our futures|a
                      new city we now call home

our roundness press against glass

we were once insignificant to ourselves

now we   shake|bow|turn   when the rain comes

left eye let's go first   right follows

crying enters the room upon exiting us

stop saying sorry|stop hurting me|stop & look both ways

i beg a man   pain becomes

an organ in the body|shadow standing in bedroom corner|devoted

after explosions
                    above|beside|in us

this world turns into a world sustained by   touching|the
                                                    rich staying
                                                    rich|violence

in this version fire eats   our abusers'
                                                    hands|the
                                                    memory
                                                    hunger
                                                    leaves|silence.

a mighty long time

children cannot forget
the way adults make them
feel. what they'd do
wrong in their sleep, they wept
for a mighty long time.
what they'd do
wrong while eating. they wept
for a mighty long time.
cannot forget the way
my not-mother made me
silent. i held my sister's hand
in the invisible kind of way,
with eyes. we wept
in plastic chairs, unmoving,
for a mighty long time.
were not brave enough to kick or shout or
kill. our abusers
did not outlive us.
they came to teach
pain.

double u, double d

we need a
wang dang doodle
a lawn chair holding
high waists
cousins racing sacks
across the yard, just a
few feet away
a pound cake offers itself
in glazed slices
there's lemonade
tea sweet as niceness
have some
save it for later
in some foil
fix a plate
hug your young necks
around one another
as swans do in summer
remember home
in its sunlight
with its warm prayer
waiting, just waiting
for the weight
of you.

for Kendrick

Assata saint to some Black folks,
Lifts fist. She who once rocked gravity
spurned Afro, breaks from prison
Did to the police what they often do to us.
Locked scalp natural, rolled fine.
They found Kendrick Johnson's cadaver
inside a gym mat.
Locs never hung so unnaturally
On a basketball court's floor
in Lowndes County.

the flower will make its debut
when everyone is dying

The flower
will make its debut when everyone is dying.
when the boy i love cannot find enough room in his jeans
    to disappear.
The daisies
will stay after he has fled
his body in search of a new nation.
In his new country he slips on wide legged jeans   taps
    formaldehyde
                behind his ears
                taps it to *hislipshisarmshiships hislegshisasshischest*
Do not call him Black or beautiful.
Call him a question pinned to the cement.
                Call him the preamble to heaven.
                Even Flower Boy would be nice.
                Call him when there is no answer.

would you kill God too?

some women will not arrive in springtime
to lay in the bluegrass of kentucky
one will die in the arms of her lover
inside the hallway of their home
he will look desperately for mercy
to show up unannounced as the bullets did just minutes before
hell hot metal shot into the walls
they coughed gypsum
in four hundred years you never knocked before entering
never entered without leaving a breath undone or a body taken
bending brief and begging for a better way to die
we bury our babies as you polish your badges
break batons over our beloveds' backs
officers
cosgrove
mattingly
hankison
how many nights have you hid the stench of homicide
tucked it in the farthest pockets of your dreams
do you explain this to your children
did you tell them the blood on your shoes belonged to a Black girl
or is she not worth mentioning
did you make a mirror out of her blood
did you stand in it
God was in the room when you made a massacre
out of someone's child

how long does a man daydream about murder
before his fingers find a gun
did the clouds resemble smoke on march 13th
what does the sky before a murder look like
officers did you see the sun set
was God standing at the horizon
did you want to reach out and kill Her too
would you kill God too
some women will not arrive in springtime
to lay in the bluegrass of kentucky
some will survive to swing the steel
of a switchblade to warn your necks
no dying happens tonight
no prisoners will be taken

boy falling

when did you know? a second after
my hand brushed against yours
      like oriole wings touched by wind? maybe,
when we missed eyes on purpose.
did we think the air would crack like ice?
      did you know? the clothes did not keep
you covered. bold blue Dodgers cap
pulled down did not blot your smile.
              so how
did it feel escaping the dark
corners of your home?
      what can you do? look away
a quarter inch to the right
& miss the entire play of your life: one boy falling
      in love with another boy. i'm the boy who knows
when God is hanging in the air.
we drove across time
      to look at each other. it was too hot
to wear shirts. it's always the cotton
getting in the way. wooden bats,
            pass like boys
through wind connect
at opposite ends
           of a man's desire.

adjust your hips

God,

    i'm thankful
    for the dew on the grass.
    for the praying mantis hidden there.
    for the hungry bird gathering the green meal into its beak.

Heavenly Father,

    you feedeth them. am i not much better than they?

God,

    i'm thankful
    for the twig the fowl found you in.
    for the branch bringing it into its bark like birth in reverse.
    for the leaf being a generous force.

O' oxygen occupying my lungs.
O' Lazarus whistled back through his body's keyhole.
O' Renisha meaning reborn.
O' in a sec she yet had been murdered.

O' spectacle of the bee's belly upturned below the plum tree.
O' dragonfly drinking dew off railroaders' lunch pails.
O' a time a Tennessean boy placed teeth in me.
O' what must whiskey gums warn us of?
O' familial spat flattened into laughter.
O' unsayable pleasure, metered into moans.
O' tongue touching like a tiger's whisker on the pockmarked
    back of a lover.

   for it is God who works in you.

God,

    i'm thankful
    for the preaching scar.
    for it being a temple of sound beyond sorrow.
    for muscle resting on bone.

O' you who saw the farthest into me.
O' my wailing made room for another sound.
O' midnights mentioning Janet Jackson cooing,
cause ima be the queen of insomnia.
O' fag hips high-fiving hands hanging by bent wrists.
O' relief runs tonic rivers onto my tongue: peppermint,
    feverfew, rosemary.
O' haunted hip traced by a no longer lover.
O' on time angel's instruction: *arch your back.*
O' adjust your hips heavenward.
O' August of '92 and '48.
O' Fred, you panther of a man.
O' everything felt possible with you here.

    uphold the cause of the poor and oppressed.

God,

    i'm thankful
    for Imani's grandma shaking a sugar sky over a cradle
        of cornflakes.
    for you, father.
    for you, mother.
    for the tambourine's terror tearing up silence.
    for you, love.
    for you, windgripper.
    for you, tornado wind.

        for the whirlwind and storm and the clouds
        dusting your feet.

ain't dying

ain't dying today
not on the wheels of Ford
Honda
Toyota
the new Kias
are nice but a nigga
barely making rent
ain't dying
in my home
in my thirties
forties
fifties
sixties
seventies
or eighties
or in a conversation
with white folks obsessing over
guns
anti choice
braids in Black girls' hair
carrying all of me back
to bed tonight
slanted tooth and arched brows
ain't dying
or getting close to it
ain't tearing the skin
or the fat
of my bottom lip

won't be a bloody mess for no one
i am nobody's dinner
unless i want to be
back won't bend into a bench
dying is simply a song today
and i can't remember the lyrics
won't ask siri
she only knows the shit we tell her
ain't dying today
going to fuck my man instead
and let him fuck me
fuck the police
fuck gravity and everything else holding niggas down
dying ain't happening today
taking all of myself
breath and body back to bed
save the plot
your sympathies
the shovel
the eulogy
save both of your faces
for tomorrow
if tomorrow ever decides
to come.

begging

The tip. Calls begin,
on God, for daddy. Couldn't pray
but we connected our hands, faithful.
Past few years pulled out tears
and glossed the day dark. There weren't any
real flowers in Hot Sauce Larry's house,
plastic paradise. Made out of begging paradise
changed hues, blueberry black
to the other side of the apricot. The drip
rolling down arches positioned,
still pointing the moon in its feral eye.

fragile things

Half dead
Pink pansies
Without ego
Watch from across
The pool.
Perpendicular
Fairy lights float.
Impressive
In darkness.
Small like a worm's beating
Heart.
Things we'd call
Fragile.
Things we'd be instructed to hold
With both hands if we were children still.
This thing
Powering into
Eventual electric depletion. The sun has gone
When you say, I am owed an apology.
A ghost snail slides by.
A black cat sleeps.
Love, tenuous, in this instant
swings.
The lights wink.
Nodding comes from those faultless flowers.
Nodding comes from me.
Sorry, I say.
I'm sorry.

water we share

Xícaro, silver, two shots, the tall one says to Charlie
the bartender, reaching to retrieve what his hard work has
earned him. his hard work has earned him an affection
for small things that scar his throat. tiny daggers. truth is, he's a
regular—every Friday he searches for the fresh face at the bar,
one that has eyes bright with the right amount of loneliness.
eyes that have not blinked upon his begging for *just one more.*

the tall one, all joked out, rocks & raises liquid tank after
liquid tank, passing battalions of sorrow to his friend &
they say: *cheers*, the same way men say *sorry* or *this is the last
time* when they actually mean *until you catch me again* on a
different day with an older but no wiser heart. the short one
coughs & laughs & is laughed at & they pat each other on the
back like men who have more regret than joy & inch by inch
their shoulders slump into each other like a god in genesis
pressing the powder of worlds together. the mud. the rock.

the water we share is unlike this iced wall they fall over. we
touch to touch, allowing skin to be skin—to sweat, to sing, to
stretch and shine. so, when C, or K, or J or N and you leave
a baptism spilling down my knuckles, I remember the days
this toast would have only but one voice & two sets of fingers
& a damn good song with the bridge being the best part & a
seventeen-year-old me searching for proof that each of you
exist, begging a jukebox in Anniston, Alabama, *one more—
please, just one more shot.*

already flesh

We know what is true,
Christ did not destroy the stone.
He rolled it.
Turned over on a Sunday, I met a boy's back
beginning an early morning beg: *claw at me here.*
His nose carries a hook a jeweler once knew.
Believe it or not the men grew gorgeous
after I stopped looking for them
To be perfect
We can make love without the beds
Of our fingers being stripped of extra skin; the manicurist
Means well: *your girlfriend is a lucky one.*
Laughter is a lamb's bleat from my mouth.
The boy slides like breath out of my bed.
He walks across the floor and it groans like a dying god.

the leash

I knew you were in a daunted place
When the dog you call disobedient
Dashed through the grass, unwilling
To lope back into his kennel. He is your darling
Show pony, the glitter young girls pat
Their eyelids with.
Your marginalized reality has made him meditative.
He pretends his bowels are filled just to sniff
Fresh suburban air.
He crafts a plan to leave you exhausted,
Greater than your boss's efforts or the men on Grindr asking,
Are you a bottom? Are you mobile?
The leash is your only control.
The dog is how you punish yourself.
Shades of earth color skin you are delighted to call light.
There's a bruise there you cannot see
With the squint of human eyes.

between boys

Look how the walls match your sadness
Brown bricks nibbling air.
How long have you been sitting there?
Slouched in stretched leather
Watching twenty-somethings swap promises
In long lengths of laughter. You remember
Having someone to watch the end of the world with.
When Google announces the Alaskan Kelp Forest is dying
You mentioned wanting to photograph sea otters:
They hold hands to keep from drifting apart.
That is no more than the distance between boys
Out there sitting thigh-close on a bench.
Neither can see your spine curled like a cat while you sneer
At the delight they both share.
Look at yourself, so sullen. You are sure
Nothing about true love is being said.
As the boys stand and walk separate ways
One looks back as if he's tying a knot
In the space between them. You lean back
From the window, holding your breath, waiting
For the other to do the same.

that one uncle
we all know

the wasps are angry drunks
much like men standing around
half full cocktails humming
with barbarity
dissolving secrets
in nightclubs and cookouts
we all know one uncle
whose laughter shuffles
behind ears elders
call wet
he plates heads on
pillows in unlit rooms right
before they
fall.

asking for miracles

I hear him say underneath his breath: *i'm dropping off your sweater*
the orange one with the pocket so big I planned on placing
    our futures inside;
the bullmastiff not yet bought, milk on baby's breath,
    our giggling fagfriends doing eight counts at our wedding. He
    does not say what I need to hear: *I did not wait in the rain*
    with you.
He can't look me in the eyes without thinking how long I held
    another man's hand
before telling him. Our anniversary unballooned & drained
    of its confetti. He finds himself asking for miracles; for the
    tumor to shrink in his mother's breast, for the picture above
    his bed to swing counter clockwise, bringing his ghost lover
    back, for water to rinse the dirt off the body exhumed from
    the grave. He hears me say underneath my breath: *someone's*
    gotta make it out alive.

baby's breath

bowing roadside is the first omen
followed by bodies posing into memory
yellow lollipop and puckered lip
polaroids pinned on laundry lines
east of Mississippi eyes catch the sun
eyes catch the sun on occasion everything is light
candles are lit to gain God's affection
laughter is caught in mason jars
orange slices slide under the skin of chicken thighs
then fried for friends' mouths
wet with more

jellyfish eyes

the gum is lodged in your throat.
now what?
do you expire from this life
and gag into the next?
would nations be hollowed of their hunger
for violence, dollars, and other cruel currencies?
who would speak at your funeral?
is it your mother who lifts her voice
over your body for one last bedtime story?
is it your well intentioned fifth-grade teacher
quoting Barack Obama, forgetting you're
a communist?
would your final thought be
everyone is going to laugh. the light
closes around you like jellyfish eyes.
would you be reminded of the last time death was this close,
staring you down with the focus of falcons?
you were twenty-eight when the car punched
into the driver's seat. you remembered
how to say God's name: *mama*.
how often do we think
we're dying but aren't?
how often do we paint
places with our own darkness?
you could have said *tell me more*,
to the picture maker at the market

as you held her prints.
why didn't you go over to the woman
screaming beneath her blanket? it is winter after all
and she needs someone to listen to how the world has offered
    her many betrayals.
wouldn't you want the same? for someone to see
how pain has twisted you unrecognizable?
on paper would you write,
help me!
wouldn't you pray for fingers to reach down your throat
and pull out the curse?
wouldn't you?

lady day visits
glynn county

for Ahmaud Arbery

no breeze finds home in georgia
heat rises like a maxwell whistle
breaking the sound barrier
lock the doors when the white men come
place your everythings inside the pantry
tell no one who or what you love
it might
they might survive
to see another day
dream
of a country where strange fruit ain't
a metaphor for being Black
merely melons coming into existence on vines
not bodies playing negligée
on the trunks of trees
no neck bones
cracking
no thunder
here another casket closing

butcher shop

I know how to beg for mercy.
I know the weight of loneliness
And things I touched trying to understand
Love. It hurts to live a life.
It is always asking for more.
Everything feels hollow
Then the blood comes.
A blade breaks an animal
Into smaller parts:
Shoulder, belly, loin, a head
Requested from the body.
What should we do to those killing us?
Cover them in soil alongside our cousins;
Tyre, Trayvon, Atatiana.
Bullets touched them the way men touch countries
When they believe in nothing.
Taste this pain
Flavored with the salt
Of our organs.
Half a pinch.
Small labor.
I won't ask twice.

aint neva

ain't neva left brick steps
Chi-town summers dripped sweat
ain't neva pushed down forehead knots
ain't neva pointed the finger at God
ain't neva noticed the knot not
disappearing into my skull
ain't neva abuse
ain't nothing neva wrong
with sparing the rod
child ain't neva gon remember
child ain't neva gon do nothing
bout being a child
ain't neva about words having meaning
ain't neva needing nothing from no
goddamn body
ain't neva begged a nigga to pick me
ain't neva prayed for God's hand
to move mountains.

as long as the dying
die without dignity

Throw thanksgiving sides on classical paintings
When the rent is too damn high
Throw gravy across Mona Lisa's forehead each time a fire
Consumes a forest
Lacquer Michelangelo's finest artifice with grease
From the fish fry
Be sure to bring white bread
For the statues of the dead and yet to live
Pour sweet tea on marble depictions of holy things
I'll make a playlist for the occasion
Sylvester's greatest hit:
I feel real when you touch me
I feel real when you hold me
And we'll soak our throats in tequila
While Venus sits in a puddle of Scotch
Throw Christmas dinner
On the Louvre's porcelain floor
As long as there's someone poor
As long as the dying die without dignity
Be a cliché
Throw a tomato
Throw two
Throw the cobbed corn
Throw the food on the underside
Of your boot.

danger dodge

it is dangerous to love him
to wipe tears from his eyes in a diner
we could die
for what sounds escape our mouths
in the jungle I bare my teeth
add extra edge to my eyes to protect
our untouched futures
each day we escape dying
we danger dodge
twisting open
new doors

little brown bat

is this what you've waited to hear?
that man. that man. that man too.
took me apart. piece by piece.
months marked my heartache
marching through the year remembering
at that park, on this couch, catty-cornered
against those terra cotta walls. it haunts me
having loved like this. giving everything
one needs to be sure love is being taken
seriously.
to be allowed wildness
a black bear's fluttering gaze,
little brown bat,
is this what you waited to hear?
love to me is natural.
love to me is spring.

leaving kessler

we weight
our pockets
with sunlight
spilling
through our loft windows
we walk
away suitcases
filled
with memories
&
fresh laundry
we sweep floors
we polish counters
&
listen to the cars driving by
we laugh
until each brick vibrates
into something softer
we hop
on planes
to places we will soon call
home
we know
of no greater encore
than gratitude

& oceans

oceans open up & you
pull each family member made meal onto the shore
of a freed world & the heart remains God's student.
We kneel here. Kneel with us. In our suffering.
Gris-gris: gold ring, revolution
Tattooed neckside. It's the thug in me.
Folded in fagskin,
Crooked tooth juju
& all I will ever hear
is my name said whole.
Hole in the trickster's jar.
Hole in the demon's scheme.
Hole in the shoulder meant for
The heart.
Touch &

Acknowledgments

Earlier versions of these poems appeared in the following journals and publications: *TIME*, *Stonecoast Review*, *Flyway*, *Allium*, *wildness*, and *Rust & Moth*.

Endless gratitude to Cave Canem, ForKeeps Books, 1977 Books, 100 WEST Artist & Writer Residency, Emory University Arts & Social Justice Fellowship, Paintlove, ArrayNow, Rebellion Writing Salon, and the community of writers who gathered in my home, around my Artedi Travertine table, with the polaroids of James Baldwin tucked under the glass.

Without the following and many more, these poems would be adrift in the wind. May we continue to be witnesses to each other. My love abounds:

Willette Lofton, Natalie Lauren Sims, Kelsey Jones, Alysia Harris, Dartricia Rollins, Rosa Duffy, Renault Verone, Jericho Brown, Dominic Williams, Keith Northcutt, Osaze Stigler, Miles Freed, Cadarius Parks, Stephen Smith, Joi Lindsey Garrett, Rasheed Tillman, Shamann Meadows, Joshua McCoy, Cole Arthur Riley, Corwin Malcolm Davis, Amyra León, Jeanine Anderson, Ava DuVernay, Sydney A. Foster, Donovan Ramsey, Blessitt Shawn Bryant, Dillon Nettles, Ashley Edwards, Ashley Pugh, Rodney Grimes, E.H., Swathi Shanmugasundaram, Vincent Davis*, Brian Ellison, Shawn Michael Craig, Caleb Seales, Simone Johnson, Remica Bingam-Risher, Daniel Jackson, Kondwani Fidel, Devin Allen, Daniel Summerhill, Jasmine

Reid, Keyo Stinson, Leah Brundidge, Amelia Quinn, Frederick Hampton, Andre Fields, Ashley M. Jones, Geneva Watford, Erin Ferguson, Brian Cornelius, Joseph Isabell, Malik Khalid, Joseph Solomon, Brea Baker, Toccara Smalls, EL Chisolm, Austin Willingham, Nathan Wallace, Sydnee Williams, Josh Wilson, Mr. John Blanding, Kier Garner, Terrell Patrick, Charisse Holmes, Michael Latt*, Dior J. Stephens, Raymond Antrobus, Chen Chen, Saleem Hue Penny, Nome Patrick Emeka, Nduta Waweru, Gustavo Aldolfo Aybar, Christopher Rose, Sa Whitley, D. Colin, Fanny Brewster, Vonkeisha Gibson, Imani Davis, Mia S. Willis, Ashlee Haze, Adan Bean, Courtney Faye Taylor, Aurielle Marie, William O'Neal, Glenn Kaino, Yvonne Agim, Eleanor Beason, Duriel E. Harris, Tracie Morris, Janice Harrington, Phillip B. Williams, Jose Vazquez, Melanie Morgan, Forrest Evans, Lakerri Mack, Phyllis Williams, Jamillah Bell, Nigel Shelby*, Chevon Guthrie, Shekrina A. Roberts, my Montgomery family, my godchildren Jasilynn and Zakai. Alice Smith: I had "I Put a Spell on You" on repeat.

Thank you Kent Wolf and Catherine Tung for reading these poems and believing in them.

Notes

The italicized lines in "right hooks" are from "Alright" by Kendrick Lamar and "Ivy" by Frank Ocean.

"for Tae" is for my classmate Antavious Billingslea.

The italicized line in "language" is from "Wildfire" by John Mayer featuring Frank Ocean from the album *Paradise Valley* (Columbia Records, 2013).

"for Kendrick" is for Kendrick Johnson, who was murdered in Lowndes County and has yet to receive justice.

"would you kill God too?" is for Breonna Taylor, originally commissioned by Ava DuVernay.

The italicized line in "adjust your hips" is from "No Sleeep" by Janet Jackson.

The italicized lines in "as long as the dying die without dignity" are from "You Make Me Feel (Mighty Real)" by Sylvester.

About the Author

© Wulf Bradley

W. J. Lofton, a Chicago-born poet and multimodal artist, is the author of *A Garden for Black Boys: Between the Stages of Soil and Stardust*. His work explores the intersections of race, class, and gender while focusing on Black queer men's attempts at intimacy and the tensions and wonders of boyhood. Lofton has received fellowships from Cave Canem and Emory University. A recipient of Ava DuVernay's LEAP Grant, he has published work in *Time*, *wildness*, *Obsidian*, and *Scalawag*. Raised in Alabama, he now calls Atlanta, Georgia, home, where he co-curates Rebellion: A Writing Salon.